SKEDADDLE

Skedaddle

JOHN LEVETT

PETERLOO POETS

First published in 1987
by Peterloo Poets
2 Kelly Gardens · Calstock · Cornwall PL18 9SA

© 1987 by John Levett

ISBN 0 905291 82 4

Printed in Great Britain by
Latimer Trend & Company Ltd, Plymouth

ACKNOWLEDGEMENTS are due to the editors of *Antigonish Review, Encounter, Honest Ulsterman, Literary Review, London Magazine, London Review of Books, Outposts, New Statesman* and *Times Literary Supplement* in whose pages many of these poems first appeared.

Cover photograph: Milky Way (Pleiades in Taurus) by courtesy of ZEFA, Düsseldorf. (Photo by Jack Novak.)

Contents

A Piece Of Cake

I came home late to find you gone,
The party over, floor swept clean,
Wet crockery stacked on its side,
Each good intention magnified.
The hard-edged kitchen hummed and shone;
Quite nakedly along their bone
A pork chop and a lamb chop lay
Among the shrink-wrapped canapés,
While mirrored in obsessive squares
A bowl of barely balanced pears
Leaned forward and colluded in
Each separable brown and green.
That isolated wedge of cake,
So self-contained I thought it fake,
Stood on the fridge and could have been
A Hockney or a late Soutine;
Its thin, acrylic stripe of jam
And matted cells of sponge became
All heightened fact, transfused detail,
Distinctly and absurdly real.
I turned to see your simple note,
The empty hook that held your coat,
Your fragile gift, the washing-up,
Each saucer on each gleaming cup,
And propped against reflective tiles
Your rings and contraceptive pills.
All summer I had wondered how
Exactly we had got that far,
And now I think of how you are,
Your finger's tell-tale band of skin
That each warm day is darkening.

S D I

Ten miles above the tits at St. Tropez
A satellite's remote, panoptic eye
Is tracking us and quietly waiting for
The gesture that could culminate in war;
You scratch your nose, I finish my ice-cream
And screw the silver paper in the sand.
Your milky skin is tanning like a dream.
That ultra-violet shadow is my hand.
The camera rolls on, its frozen lens
Picks out the agriculture of the Fens
Then swaps the filters for the infra-red
Cupolas of beleaguered Leningrad.

You shift and turn, your shoulder-blade could be
The smooth lid on some high-tech armoury
And fear stirs in the craters that begin
To open on my weakly English chin.
White clouds wind like a turban round the peaks
That top the Himalayas, and the sun,
Its compost of alchemical techniques,
Transmutes the globe and lets us focus on
Calcutta pullulating with its poor,
The psychopaths that bleed El Salvador
The human tides of Tokyo and then
The terrifying silence of Phnom Penh.

The earth speeds up, its shrunken polar caps
Like parachutes tumescently collapse,
The tilting coasts of snow give way to ice
Then bergs of light on Asian belts of rice.
At eight you plan to have the hotel fix
Your hair and come to meet me in the town,
Its chill and its salinity that pricks
And tightens up a skin that's nicely brown:
Those stars we hope to drink beneath tonight
Are pledged to North America, that white
Deliberative brilliance even now
The obsolescent hardware of The Plough.

Bunker

Day breaks and the night steams North,
Its pitch dark barges heading for
Cape Rigor and the Land of Truth,
Perfection's speculative glare;
The seas ice over and preserve
Their endlessly refractive coast,
An empty and eternal curve,
Light packed against the polar frost.

These August nights are nothing more
Than souped-up evenings, sweat-soaked sheets,
Or coming to on someone's floor
And morning's featherweight retreats;
And even when we die we live
Hopped up in someone's latest suit,
Pumped full of sour preservative,
Our grin set at the absolute,
For several sticky nights at least
Until we're spaded in or burn
And flames or worms or poltergeist
Snap down the lid on our return.

No wonder, then, we keep this place,
This ideal arctic of the mind,
Despite the latest U.S. base
Or half-crazed men returning blind;
No wonder that we make it white
And pure and blank, untrespassed on,
And outside time, an infinite,
Bright bunker of our own.

The Bridge At Avignon

They are dancing on the bridge at Avignon
In their Flemish clothes and clogs as good as new,
You can see their footwork flicker in the sun,
The river's almost sedimentary glow,

And from their eyes you know they are possessed,
Imprisoned by the tinkling of a tune,
Beside themselves and strangely overdressed
On this cataleptic summer afternoon.

They are dancing and the bridge is made of stone,
The silence is hypnotic and the sky
Is blue above the delta of the Rhône
Where the ancient, sunlit currents multiply.

But no one looks and no one really cares,
The antipopes, the prostitutes, the thieves,
The cripples with their questionable wares,
The retrospective flourish of the trees

Whose dusty branches let the sunlight fall
Then hold it just this inch above the ground
Where the mediaeval future seems to stall
As the little song goes round and round and round.

Company

Cold air swings through the trees
On ropes of mist today
And ripe anatomies
Close up and fold away,

A wry and sketchy leaf
Turns on its skeleton,
The chill preserves my breath,
Late sun pickles a stone.

Rain idles on the air
And skips the wood to fuss
The edgy pavements where
Its sullen impetus

Is carried on the back
Of gravity into
The artificial lake,
Its unprotesting blue.

The traces of a fire
Have sealed into a sweet
Black pabulum to tar
The ground beneath my feet.

Now everywhere I turn
Was tenanted before;
The ashes itch to burn,
Flames roll across the floor.

Agoraphobia

Here comes the wind with a cloud on its arm
Waltzing high over these acres of warm
Pasture and stubble and joining the trees
In their spirited choreographies.

How should we greet it? Is raising a hat
Considered uncivil on broadlands or flat
Levels of meadow that fold up to where
The shape of a hill makes the wood disappear?

Surely it's spotted us, lifted above
The details of trivial landscape by love
And joined to each other by hands that have grown,
Under the weather, a lattice of bone.

Fear takes you from me like straw on the wind,
The old and abandoned nest of the mind
Goes scattering over promiscuous weald.
Sunshine. Your back's inappropriate shield.

A Departure

On this mild island even rocks'
Slow tolerance cannot ignore
The humped and unassertive shapes
Of gunboats anchored off the shore.
Now only changing weathers bring
New prospects or some second glance;
A damaged cliff face altering
October's sharp exhuberance,
The slack commotion of a sea
Withdrawing as each fumbled wave
Claps out into transparency
Not even sunlight can retrieve.
Departing tourists stand in line,
The ferry sidles to and fro,
Its decks awash, a submarine
Goes down and all our futures go
With what she carries, ordnance, lives,
Partitions of recycled air,
Our stockpiles and preservatives
Submerged and heading God knows where.

Skedaddle

It is midnight and I have let in the cat.
I stand at the door and examine the stars
And his shadow skedaddles between my feet,
His Egyptian head and four white paws
Joining me in the cosmic sweep,
The ritualistic good night sniff,
Our sense of eternity on the cheap,
The infinite held like a handkerchief.
The moon goes bowling through the air
On its desolate, elliptic spree,
And I watch as its sodium craters flare
From Crises to Tranquility,
From the Sea of Clouds to the Sea of Rains,
From the tumble of one dull red star
To the starboard light of a late night plane
For Archangel or Panama,
Cresting the atmospheric storms
With its T.V. sets and embargoed arms
And the whole technological can of worms.
Implausibly collapsing star
We, like you, are waiting for
Whatever political key unlocks
Pandora's thermonuclear box,
That Freud, Saussure and Levi-Straus,
Gorbachov and Mickey Mouse,
Islam and the Catholic Church
All join hands as the planets lurch,
And Ptolemy's error and Pascal's doubt,
And the earth and its complicated crust
Will all, like us, go sputtering out
In a puff of unenlightened dust.
A radar dish picks up a breeze,
Black lupins wave beside the gate
Where a clump of Thyme and Japanese
Miniatures proliferate.
I close the door and shoot the bolt

And fork the meat into the bowl.
In caves of ice the currents jolt,
The cryogenic fossils howl
For the quick release, the coming heat
No private life can sublimate.
Slowly, in the dark, I climb the stairs,
Undress and slide beside you into bed
And when I stir your pressure reassures,
You turn and find my shoulder with your head,
Then roll away, convinced that I am there,
That asking any more would be absurd.

Snap

Slowly the film rolls on, then jogs, then stops.
You are standing by a wall in Kent;
behind you spreads a great house from a book.
You are about to step into a photograph,
a cold and formal element,
a classic close, a seal of black and white,
where one half is the afternoon
and the other half not quite.
Curved and fixed your smile will stay
stone dead inside this no-man's land,
its colour bled away. I press the switch
and catch you with your eyes half closed,
your hair blown back, your mouth awry;
and when the film rolls on again
you start up like a figure from
a Buñuel or Eisenstein. No one I know,
at least not yet. If that's to come
it's still to be invented. Take your pick,
and though you choose concernedly be quick,
for everything is settled in a leap,
a tone of voice, a gesture or a face,
and all the rest is background, like this house,
its big doors locked, its spreading creepers rich
with unlit windows where the light has crashed.

Chorus Line

Your tank is full of hyperactive fish
And their movements give the brilliant game away
As twists of shadow coil like liquorish
Across the path of disappointed Koi
And red and silver guppies come and go
Erupting on the vegetative screen.
Freshwater and its basement studio,
A study in depressive submarine.

The eye survives enclosure and mutates,
Makes out among varieties of shade
The beginnings of a spectrum that locates
Dull bursts of blue, a violet arcade.
The less we have the more we see of it.
We pare things down, reduce them, say, to this
Warm-water tank and thin flourescent light,
Then settle to the slow analysis;
The painstaking removal, one by one,
Of all the separable elements,
Forestial and Amazonian
The tributary each species represents,
Their colouration and their mating types,
The quickening reminder of each fin,
Their habits and their slim, distinctive shapes,
Their warm and speculative origins.
And finally we know them off by heart,
And then we know before we have to think,
As I, poor fish, can instantly make out
Your face from all those other shades of pink.

Beanfeast

Considering the way we live,
The slim chance that we may not be
Bombed out on starch and additive,
De-toxified or gluten-free,
Its not surprising chaos grows
And violence feeds a yawning want,
Dosed up on cellular lactose,
Wheat flour and antioxidant;
Destabilized by fish and chips
And wrapped and paste-injected pies,
The crude fuel of apocalypse,
Our failure to metabolize.
Plagued as I am throughout this Lent
With images that still adhere
Through moribund advertisement
To smoke and photogenic beer,
I grow confused and come to wish
For non-addictive, childish need,
The sacrament of liquorice,
The penitence of aniseed.
We eat too much and what we eat
Is poisonous, no longer real,
The candied fruits are incomplete
Without their shot of cochineal;
Our meat and fish so deeply fried
They merge into the cardboard plate
As unrelieved, emulsified
Monosodium glutamate.
Meanwhile those millions in the East,
Unconscious of our ends and means,
Our technicological beanfeast,
Our fun and junk-food gelatines,
In black and white and wave on wave
Reproach us with their single look
And while collectively they starve
We separately choke.

The Really Bad News

(for Peter)

Should some silicone genie, some waterproof sprite,
Some Ariel split from asbestos or chrome,
Once grant me the cash to see you all right
And to usher you into an unmortgaged home,
And then give me three wishes, the first one would be
Your clear and emphatic victory
In the 100 and 200 metres at
The Southern Counties Junior Championships of 1998.
But that, I know, is too much to ask,
Too specific, too local to ever come true,
So I'll cover myself and just wish you good luck
With whatever ambitions you happen to choose,
Or whichever small talent, let's say, chooses you;
And then, as a final hedge against luck,
Against politics, love and the really bad news,
That tough, overworked, unrenewable knack
Of learning how to lose.

21

The Watering Can

This rose would fountain rust
If it were ever used,
An oxidised disgust,
Its beaten zinc is bruised.

A seeth of mineral
Makes waves inside the rim,
Old water's rise and fall
Remeasuring the whim

Of balance and sunlight
One August afternoon,
The lunatic delight
Of spilling with the moon,

The pressure at the tap,
The lift of emptiness,
The buoyancies that shape,
Contingencies that press.

Propped drunk against a wall,
Rehearsing some old tilt,
I watch my shadow fall
And fill it to the hilt.

A Fortune

The cliff face sways, the pebble tilts,
July wades in on sunlit stilts,
Beneath their tides' impulsive weight
The concave seas decelerate
And fall away to slug and blur
Where blue anxieties occur
And white horizons stretch to press
Perspectives into nothingness.

Along the pier, past the arcade,
As scraps of inshore music fade,
The fortune teller, far from land,
Consults your vulnerable right hand
And traces in unfolding lines
Our own imaginary designs;
To you a brilliant child, to me
Success, good health, ability.

Dismissing you she yawns and then
Turns out to watch the fishermen,
Their angled and attentive lines
Antennae as the swell divines
A passing ship. She stands to watch
Their heads bent for the sudden catch,
But nothing comes beyond a laugh
Preserved in some old photograph.

Now on that still, complacent coast
The fruit is an astonished ghost
Inside red wine that bears the year
We walked along the vanished pier.
Nothing happened. Or, at least,
Not as she said, or as we wished;
Our lives trailed on the things that she
Once offered us so casually.

Los Angeles

Miniaturized on Astroturf
The golden athletes jump and run
As rolling static breaks like surf
Across the saturated screen;
A mythic Californian sun,
Boosting the colour, burns unseen.

In Greenwich, London, heavy rain
Has come to nothing. On the Thames
A tug hoots to an empty crane,
And for as far as the eye can see
The wharves with their defective names
Litter the estuary.

Tonight, like every other night,
Out through the cold and back,
A microelectric satellite
Dodges the stars and reconnects
The unphased image with the docks'
Bronchitic sound effects,

While Coliseums, white and clean,
Stuck in their cubes of coastal haze,
Their tides and fogs of gasoline,
Are bounced across the hyperspace
And only the speed of light delays
The smile on each miniature winner's face.

This is our future, this is why
Remote, evangelistic, bright
America is riding high
On space-wars, sport and politics,
And all the things that won't go right
That a little cash can fix.

Old Holborn

Adrift in suburban gardens
High peonies balloon,
The martin and the jay rehearse
Their thirty-first of June,

Clematis threads its argument
On trellises of blue,
The bald-faced moon ashamedly
Slips down the avenue

As six o'clock evaporates
And pond weeds coil and choke,
And dogged grass perks up again,
And monkey puzzles smoke.

Beyond the shouldered labyrinth
Of crescent, close and lane,
The cinder clicks its fingers,
The wind dives down each drain,

And plexiglass and chromium
Encode a fitful sun,
A futility of signals,
A desolate dry-run.

With pinks and flags the cityscape's
Perimeters are trim,
But certainties, like heavy men,
Make chances seem so slim,

As one stands by his window-box
And hangs this bluish net
Above the match that shakes to light
His dodgy cigarette.

The Pastel

The river bank in pastel. Here a boy
Supported by a staff conducts his geese,
A solid carthorse balanced like a toy
Is nosing through idealistic grass,
Beyond them, and too good to be quite true,
Lies flat, undifferentiated blue.

A steamer with a scribble of brown smoke
Transfixes the horizon while above,
Like second thoughts, absorbent clouds invoke
The threat of unreal weather turning rough.
Our pleasure under glass, a footloose day
That not a single detail will betray.

The things that matter stay outside the frame.
The sun, for instance, turning on the glare,
The unimportant artist's christian name,
The modest smudge of urban atmosphere,
And further still the shadows that explore
The empty room, the slowly closing door.

Quantum

Snow fills the heath,
It brief, off-white,
Inventive flakes
Distort the night.
I watch a drift
Pick up and stack
The dark onto
Its sparkling back
And then slope off
And dump its weight
On roofs where roads
Evaporate.

The air is cold.
A little pain
Can crumple time
Like cellophane,
And screw up space
And tear away
The shrink-wrap from
The light of day.
Thick and fast
Across the sky
The rubbished crystals
Multiply.

Too chilled to stand
I climb the hill,
Having one more
Hour to kill;
Wind operates
Its dummy trees
Impersonating
Galaxies:
The lights of cars
Are lost among
The failures of
Its cosmic song.

The sudden snow's
White gravity
Has duped the grass,
Its polar spree
Reflects the night's
Celestial hive
Where all the strange
Dimensions thrive,
Where all the senses
Hitch a ride
And nothing is
Personified.

Meanwhile, above,
Our own stars glow,
Platonic bits
Of ideal snow;
Internal
Subatomic spin
Preserves their flashy
Origin.
Dumped with light
On board the bus
Pale strangers flare
Like bits of us.

Luxury

The separate banks are beggared now below
The cold, synthetic luxury of snow
And like some beautiful device
The river stalled beneath the ice
Must balance on its stoppered undertow.

A rook tears from the branches of a tree,
The shadows scutter, echoes jag and spree
Along the winds that lend their weight
To gravity and isolate
The silences that brew such energy.

Somewhere beyond our pale, untroubled hedge
A motorway rears up into a bridge,
Confidingly the headlamps glance
Across the unopposed advance
Of dusk and dip, absorbed into the ridge.

Fast moving clouds allow us to observe
The sharply potent distance hug its curve,
And then the frail phenomena,
The coming moon, the unslung star,
And finally the darkness we deserve.

I draw the curtains, turn into the gloom
And guyed by reassurances presume
Your presence in the empty sift
Of dresses and the things you left,
Your brushes and your mirror and your comb.

Toys

A costermonger's stall
With plastic fruit
Stands in the rain,
A flyweight interval
Across the blurring pane
Where damaged toys distort
July's ill-discipline.

A beige and partly torn
Old cowboy hat
Thrown by a gust
Of wind across the lawn
Has finally gone west;
A scooter with a flat
Front tyre begins to rust.

Rain fills a cracked teapot,
Contrives to miss
A furless dog
Our daughter once forgot.
A trenchant rubber frog
Squats wary of all this
Inclement catalogue.

Within the warm back room
I turn to reach
The travel guide,
Expectantly resume
The chill, delusive tide,
As distances beseech
And waves and sand collide.

Zig-Zag

The chalk path zig-zags up the cliff
To an old tar road that leaves the town
And I would zig-zag with it if
You were here to go with me;
Instead I make it slowly, grown
Light-headed on the scree.
The roundabouts go round and round
On plywood platforms, greasy wheels,
And the petrifying screams are drowned
As the fizz of early puberty
Spins boys and girls head over heels
Above a solid sea,
Where winds flap unresponsive sheets
Or fold them up as spots of rain
Distort the glass and dusk completes
Another inconclusive day;
The submerged stars bob up again,
Lights glide across the bay.
The night above the town is steep,
My mouth steams like an opened flask,
The dining room is warm and cheap
And across the clouded cutlery
A voice asks things it would not ask
If you were here with me.

Mogadon

After a night of chemically assisted sleep
I draw the curtains on a sky so clear,
So flagrant in its systematic leap
Across the hedge and ditch of Cambridgeshire,
That suddenly the place is not so bad,
The landscape, so reluctant to impress,
An ideal antidote to all the wrecked
Assertions of imagined wilderness
The window frames a momentary end,
Low hills becalmed by sleeplessness, a lane
That runs along a curve of light to blend
The skyline with the quietistic fens,
While high above a tiny aircraft spins,
Its struts and tissues tightened in the breeze,
Its balsa fuselage and doped designs
Of drunken dives and sheer recoveries.
Such mornings! Pharmaceutically slow
And sealed off from the weathers that sustain
These waves of grass that luminously blow
Down hillsides of evapouring rain.

Stick Of Rock

Through twisted sticks
Of greens and blues,
The KISS ME QUICKS
And I LOVE YOUS,
The sweet knick knacks
That line the walls,
Stereoptics,
Bat and balls,
The rubber eggs,
The canned sunshine,
The female legs
In cellophane,
The plastic spade
And bucket sets,
Tinned orangeade,
Shaped chocolates,
The saccharine
And starch cigar,
The Queen, Our Queen,
In replica,
The rise and fall
Of profit, loss
Ungraspable
As candyfloss,
We join the flock
Through Kingdom Come,
Our 'Stick of Rock
Emporium'.
After the beach
And frozen drinks,
The windblown walk
Along the links,
The open bus
Around the bay,
The felt-tipped FUZZ
and I.R.A.,

The fly blown roll,
Metallic tea,
White aerosol
STUFF CND,
Official words,
KEEP OFF THE GRASS,
The wake of birds,
The modelled glass,
We're passing through
What most have missed,
The only true
Surrealist
Plan for living
That we have,
Where ashtrays sing
Of death and love,
Where rubber masks
Eavesdrop like spies
And no one asks
But someone sighs
Into the mike
Across the tide
'O I do like
To be beside
The seaside,
Beside the sea'.

The Ghost of Blériot

It isn't the rain but the theory of rain,
The idea, not the particular storm,
The concept of bubbles that brightens champagne,
The mist thrown off, not the bottle grown warm;
The unheralded ache in your jaw as the talk
Twists off into her involuntary yawn;
The cul-de-sac on the untaken walk
After the party that leads into dawn.
Exploring the streets in that mildest of Mays,
Preoccupied and inexplicably lost,
Pinched by a chill that would turn to a haze
When the sun was up and the heat came off,
It wasn't the grass but the image of grass,
The picture of smoke, not the smoke itself,
The philosophy of the unblown glass
As she reached for the mirror's repetitive shelf,
And the drink unpoured and the words unsaid
And the meeting postponed that would never take place
And the irony of the unmade bed
In the muffed readjustment of her face.
It is not what we know, or think we know,
But the things of which we are never aware
That lead us from where we mean to go
To the town where we finally reappear
With a cloud like the ghost of Blériot
Bumping over the square.

Jack-in-a-Box

Shut up, coiled in a compact box
And tethered by an anxious spring,
On call until her hand unlocks
The hinge of my astonishing,
It is for her sake that I keep
Each stunning and advertant leap
Contained so that she may not guess
The force of my preparedness

My forehead lined and knapped with fear,
Eyes wide with coarse expectancy,
Bestowing on the atmosphere
Whatever she would wish of me,
I am the shock she can't resist,
The leering exhibitionist,
The inexpensive, useful toy
Not even boredom can destroy.

She grows away from me but fright
Will bring her back and terror keep
Her eyes fixed on my stark delight
Emerging from the traps of sleep;
My simple mechanism will
Go with her as a principle
And even when it's broken stay,
With luck, to keep her company.

Plenty

What local god dispensed these stones
Dropped like aspirin in the stream
To deaden summer afternoons
With analgesic whites and creams?
And is he pleased with what we bring?
The mellowed sacrifice of cheese?
Green Tupperware whose vacuum ring
Has brought you to your knees?
How kind he was to brew this shade,
Invent this stimulating pine
To cool their cups of lemonade,
Our beakers of Italian wine.
But would he, do you think, find fault
In napkins labelled 'Hers' and 'His',
In biscuits, chocolate, lettuce, fruit,
In figurative sweet oranges?
Such plenty comforts us but he
Might think it in outrageous taste,
See proofs of our impiety
And wicked, irreligious waste.
So careful kids! And walk don't run
Too near these steep and muddy shelves
Where Airfix tubes and butane cans
And little bones dissolve.

The Natural History Museum, South Kensington

Dutiful parents, we usher our young
Through the curtain of air and the plate-glass doors
To stand in the gloom and dry out among
The widespread bones of the dinosaurs,
Then head for the worn-down stone of the stair
And terrace by brass-railed terrace ascend
To the giddy recognition we share
With each brief genetic trend;
While outside another anarchic day
Is dejectedly winding down
Through imperial trappings and urban decay
To an apron of waterlogged lawn.

This is, after all, for what it's designed,
The whole of Creation under one roof,
Religion and Art both deftly combined
With a statutory pinch of the Truth;
Where faith and cash were merged to suggest
A complex cathedral for fossil and beast,
A prodigal place and severally blessed
By architect, scientist, priest.
Today it is packed, a contemporary ark
Cast off from its rain-lashed origins,
As though God in making the light and the dark
Wasn't sure who eventually wins.

We shove past the mammals, their creaking weight
Stuffed in each glass-sided, airtight case,
Past the gold-leafed plaques that authenticate
And the fluorescent strips that erase,
Past the eyes and the bones and the horns and the wings,
Past the fish that gasp in mid-air,
Through the mythical chambers where Nautilus sings
To the heights where the tail-feathers flare,
And return, as always, to sand and to rock,
To igneous rubble, to quartz and blue tar,
To the glacial shift and atomic lock
On this chunk of a dying star.

Radiotherapy

A soft and endless loop
Of fifties music plays
Above our random group;
Well used to these delays
The tropical, lit fish,
Absorbed and pliant, move.
The name-tag on your wrist
Has isolated love.
Distraction comes too soon,
They draw lines on your breast,
Or where it once had been,
And usher you, poor guest,
Onto the corridor
Past cupboards, telephones,
Just one of many more
In functional white gowns;
Yet once inside that room
Layed out, marked up, you are
Alone, a long way from
All help and all desire.
Nowadays, thank God, the staff
Have microphones, T.V.'s.
They chat to you and laugh.
Life's little ironies.

Anniversary

Discarded petals, cabbage-whites
Fall past our ears to celebrate
Like gravity's drunk acolytes
Impossibilities of weight.

Our daughter is concerned, our son
Delighted by this sudden brush
With butterflies that one by one
Tip outwards from their startled bush

And clutter our intended stay
So thick upon the air we must
Retread the tar of mid-July
And paddle palms to readjust.

What's panic but a strict surprise?
That blemished wedding picture where
We duck as thin confetti flies
And snows across the camera.

Piano

We never heard it play, although we knew,
Like so much else, it had seen better days,
Had known a lighter touch than we could show,
Been peddled as an instrument of praise;
Had lifted someone's parlour clean above
Their dingily Victorian concerns,
Disconsolate with moonlight, sick with love,
Impassioned and uproarious by turns.
Our front room proved its final resting place,
Untended on the cold linoleum,
A monument to disappointed grace,
A casualty, its gloomy kingdom come.
We broke it up one winter afternoon
With long, unweildly hammers and a saw,
Enjoyed it too, the sudden bearing down
On all that had been sacrosanct before;
The polished top, the pale, discoloured keys,
The unexpected patternings of wire,
Sweet music and its sad redundancies
Cut down to size and ready for the fire.
Three weeks it took to burn and every night
A little more was picked up with the coal
Or balanced on the paper in the grate
To crack and spit abruptly down the scale.
The legs we saved till last, their stubborn fuel
Was resinous, reluctant, slicked with tar,
The lions carved on them motionless until
The downdraft took them upwards with a roar.

Closing Time

Tables of fake onyx,
These flames that mist the cold,
Idle gin and tonics
Ungloved hands will hold,
Sifts of fox and coney,
This surplus gleam of brass
Isolate entirely
Our lower-middle-class.

Outside, light-years away
From unattended cars,
December nights display
Expensive looking stars;
Inhuman opulence,
Celestial estates:
Deep, deep inside the gents
The damp accumulates.

How did we get this far?
The luminous saloon
Holds steady on a tar
That rocks beneath the moon;
Our footprints as we go
Are taken by the frost
Then dusted by the snow
Then covered up and lost.

Sprinters

It is spring and the sprinters are out again.
From my window I watch them sample the grass,
Neurotically stepping as though to contain
Whatever it is that makes people fast,
And limbering over the asphalt square
And rocking from foot to colourful foot,
Obsessed with speed, or at least the idea
Of speed's unachievable absolute.
To be honest, they're not really very good,
They are ragged, critically overweight,
And when they start trying their actions are crude,
Their expressions a little too desperate,
And something about them, perhaps this vain,
This repeated, impulsive attempt at speed,
Is suggestive, now it is spring again,
Of all clumsily handled need.

Anobium Hirtum

Each bible wears its token scent,
Its snuff of dust, its guarantee,
Its brewed, unhealthy testament
To genuine antiquity,
While vague collectors potter round
And dip from book to fancied book,
Uncertain between quarter-bound
Old psalters and a Pentateuch;
Find quandaries in the piled, oblique
And faded Roman letters, hear
The rustle of a Standard Greek
Releasing its bacteria.
Alive on this ramshackle stall
Religion finds a resting place,
An unhygienic festival
Of love, humility and grace,
A Babel of resistant themes
Clapped up in boards as sunlight picks
Its way along the gingered seams
And kippers each stamped crucifix.
Although their languages are dead
These leaves and spines are running wild
And what turns on them overfed,
Abundant, multiple and spoiled:
This way, perhaps, The Word plays host
And Matthew, Mark and Luke and John,
The Father, Son and Holy Ghost
Incarnate are, and nourished on.

The Snow Scene

A sudden rise of twee
And gyroscopic snow
Makes hay of gravity
Then settles to a slow

And fitful sediment
That leaves the water clear
To artfully present
Undamaged atmosphere.

Two sentries in a box
Beside a palace gate,
The detail orthodox,
The plastic intimate,

A flurried version of
That old Romantic turn,
The lives that cannot move
Traced round a Grecian Urn,

But scaled down for the age
And mass-produced to give
Our minds that lack the range
Some cheap alternative.

Invested with a weight
Beyond their substance these
Lost figures concentrate
A gift's desire to please

With each slow motion spree
Of decorative snow,
A wished catastrophe
Before the real ones blow.

Water

The radicalism of water, the way it finds its own level
Whatever the inclination or the circumstance, the way it goes
  underground
For years, patiently informing and feeding its various landscapes,
Unanxious and inaudible until
The spout-hole or the white artesian well.
The communist river, the egalitarian stream, the unselective
  estuary.
The way it simultaneously satisfies and absolves,
Baptismal or murderous, pleasurable, free.
Walt Whitman was 80% water
As also, they say, are we. It comes as no surprise
When you think of water, changeable, tumbling ambivalent
Towards its unpredictable and inconsistent ends;
The way in the sun it can seem sublime, or its dull, indecent glaze.
The way it turns and purls, eroding and reforming,
Its cargoes of unconscious fish, its mating grounds,
Its welcoming of mammals, its gasps and swells,
Its bursts of embarassing and childish delight, its domesticity
And suffocating quiet. Having known heights,
Having fallen exalted from its altitudes and fizzed
Through the collapsible cliff-face and the porous gulch
It is not overawed by class or, indeed, by size;
It could take a valley to pieces if it had a mind,
It could ruin a well-known mountain, remove enough latent power
To strand a country the size of Canada. That it doesn't
Is something we are not often enough grateful for,
And this may, in the end, be our deserved undoing.
And we in the West are especially responsible,
Belonging as we do to the bustling theocracies,
Using water for both a literal and a symbolic end,
Watching it bubble from expensive fountains, filling bottles
And cans with its aereated and coloured travesties and pissing it all
  back
Eventually. Saying it is like spirit, that it cannot be held
Except by the love of God or the elegaic tilt of gravity.

Using it to put out fires or knock down protestors
In Chicago or the Phillipines. Practical and transcendental
It could do for us tomorrow if it chose. Its fragile springs,
Its loose democracies, its confederation of unlit lakes that feed
The infant streams and rivers and the tangled tributaries,
Its liberating passage through the counties,
Its uninhibited and seemingly inconsequential progress
To the open and good-natured touch
Of its seven dangerous seas.

Dumps

A sodden mattress, gold, imploded tins,
The primly moulded torso of a doll,
The mâché of impastoed magazines,
Crocked wreckage from a rainbow or perhaps
A symptom as they slip beyond control
And all our older certainties collapse.

Society exfoliates with rust,
Centres turn to edges, shapes to mass,
Solidities exemplifying trust
We placed in the quotidian become
These dumps beyond the perfect panes of glass
That fall between environment and home.

Fey hexagons washed from a plastic ball,
A lonely glove that beckons from a tree,
The deed-box that resolves to mineral,
Stray sunshine picking over random shards,
These ask us to embrace our entropy
And all the little things we tend towards.

The Warm Estate

The ice cream van's unstable tune
Reallocates the afternoon
With notes that fall like bright and clear
Confetti on the passive ear
And stops that scarcely punctuate
Their drift across this warm estate.

Our suburb is a toyshop now
The nearby field excites the plough;
Late summer has reduced its scale
But somehow magnified detail
And so the van along the lee
Goes scattering cheap melody.

September will break up our lives,
Bring narrowing alternatives,
And curtains drawn show every house
Slowly turning serious;
Distractedly upon the gloom,
Thin lamps will hang their orange bloom.

This afternoon, perhaps the last,
The weather turns inconoclast,
The ice cream van we cannot see
Some token of its courtesy,
Exchanging for each fifteen pence
A sample of impermanence.

Packed Lunches

At one o'clock their tiny plastic chairs
Are stacked into the corners of the hall;
Brown apple cores, dead yoghurts, fibrous pears,
Like fall-out from some harvest festival,
Are scattered arbitrarily between
These ectoplasmic balls of cellophane.

Their lunch boxes are colourful and stuck
With pictures of Darth Vader, Charlie Brown,
With Snoopy in the doghouse, Donald Duck,
And Jedi in a blaze of silicone;
They tremble on their hinges or fall of,
Indignant ghosts of bright, adhesive fluff.

No space trips for their owners, no escapes,
No lighting out for some deserted star,
And trapped within their own instinctive shapes,
How gravely burdened, vulnerable they are
These sullen, antiseptic Aprils when
Grey cloud reflects the playground's bitumen.

Why Jimmy left an orange, why Yvonne
Had snapped her water biscuit into three,
Why Sussan shared her chocolate with John
But John would not share his with Rosemary;
Such mild enigmas surface and half-form
And tease us in the muddle of this room
With all the little treacheries to come.

Closedown

You watch me work at speech
Slowed down and amplified
Yet still beyond your reach,
My static slip and slide

That interval between
Two stations on the dial,
You strain at what I mean,
Not knowing makes you smile

And mistiming your guess
You nod while I still play;
My words are meaningless,
My gesturing hearsay.

It isn't only age
That leads you into this
Accumulating rage
And stray hypothesis

But partly new technique
Adopted to control
That ever present freak
The other person's will,

Responding with 'Goodbye'
As I stand up to go
And close down for the day
Love's broken radio.

Parents

The infantry of both world wars
Are swarming up the perfect slope
Your legs have made beneath the quilt,
Their faces are expressionless,
Their hand-held weapons obsolete,
Their superceeded politics
Forgotten as you roll away
And knock them all for six.
Each little plastic replica,
British or American,
Dark blue or cheap khaki,
Seems totally indifferent
As though it's our misfortune
To winter 1984
Instead of jammed and packed like them
In August '43.
Brens and mortars, automatic
Pistols, green grenades,
All fallen from the vanished hill
Into the polyester pool
Your straightened knees have made.
Our son comes in to claim them back
Theatrically cross;
He bears and cradles them away,
Grave, almost solicitous,
And angry at your careless whim
As though he is concerned for them,
As, maybe, all those years ago,
They might have been for him.

Newsflash

The sole gone cold and pushed across the plate,
The white wine in the glass she did not want,
The emerald parsley, frail and intricate,
The close walls of the dismal restaurant;
The fade across the tablecloth, the heat
From three bad candles swollen in the gloom,
The separating shadows that compete
With unlit flesh and bone for elbow-room,

And then the flash, a wave across the wall,
The gasp of wickerwork, the split tureen,
The dust-filled and the clockless interval
Around each jagged, forensic smithereen:
The keepsake photograph, just inches tall,
Blown up and reassembled on the screen.

Housework

Inside the house his cup
Was still half full, the plates
Propped with the washing up
Until he might come back,
Reproaching her they wait
Beside the draining rack.

Clogged sugar in the bowl,
Thin butter on the knife,
His habits and his whole
Routine stopped with his heart,
His swaying over life
Right from her meagre start,

And now she must preside
Over this poor estate,
A dull pain at her side
And dryness at her throat;
Her own heart detonates
Somewhere inside her coat.

The cold food in the fridge,
The too familiar shoes,
The expert rubber wedge
He cut to hold the door,
Whatever she will choose
Comes back as once before,

And slowly he returns
With things she cannot do.
Beside a vase of fern
She cries above the mess
Perhaps because it knew
His vanished clumsiness.

Charms

She hurries past the smaller shops to try
'That heap of lucky charms before they've gone',
Deliberating awkwardly to buy
Two silver skulls, a golden skeleton.

We cross to where the sea corrupts the beach
And lie among the people and their warm
Broadcast of accumulating speech
That carries on the tide's delusive calm.

She's beautiful. I watch her moving free
From corduroy and cotton in a swift
And peach-complected sinuosity
That glistens with unwrapping like a gift.

Behind us float the rows of sullen shops,
Beyond us agitation, sunlight, dust,
And all around a breeze that gently props
So many things to lay our charms against.

Laughter

Their voices uncontrolled,
Their sunburned muscles hard
Against the grey and gold
Of beach and promenade,
The local youngsters drift
Through light that interests
This boy's abandoned shirt,
That girl's inventive breasts.

At thirty comes the fear
That negligence is lost;
Our bodies start to wear
Each posture like a cast,
Discretion brings its cramp
And dignity its fuss
To little shifts that vamp
The once spontaneous.

My children thread and turn
Through shuttled waves, or dance
On spindles of the sun
As bigger tides advance,
While I remain composed
In shadow on a chair,
My adolesence closed,
My dreams in ill-repair,
And gracelessly resist
This sudden need to have
Some reason to exist,
Some formulary of love.

I hug a can of beer
And lean toward the light,
Soft puffs of cloud adhere,
Taut surfaces invite;
Against the grey and gold
Of beach and promenade
Down steps the sounds unfold,
Through walls the voices fade
And smaller talk invests
And nods and smiles divert
Those inattentive breasts,
That white, abandoned shirt.

Here Be Dragons

Those soft and fat-cheeked cherubim
That blow the clouds across the maps
And stir the seas where islands swim
And into which the cliffs collapse,
Have given up the ghost it seems,
The ragged corners of their world
Are crumpled into browns and creams
Where incredulity lies furled.

'Here be Dragons.' Well, its true,
Surviving our accepted science;
Beneath the sky's commercial blue,
Its bright flags of convenience,
A sea-cow or a coelacanth
Is netted by a rusty ship
And shimmies off its beauty with
A bloodless and convulsive flip.

We live in a resilient age.
Caught in a squall of acid rain
Curved isobars describe a cage
Barometers and screens maintain;
Vague distances no longer blur
And superstitions won't unleash
Those legends that with Mercator
Lie beached on shelves of microfiche.

On Lizard Point a five year old
Looks down with a seraphic grin,
Her hair a charitable gold
Of dark, barbaric origin;
She puffs and shreds a dandelion,
A minor wonder, while below,
Caught lightly on the seeds' decline,
Obedient, the white yachts go.

A Footnote to MacNeice

I've watched your syllables, their dance
With detail over dissonance
In patterns that both old and new
Simultaneously construe
Tradition and what might come next,
Spontaneous, rehearsed, perplexed;
The stylish way you could discard
Old theories and the avant-garde
Effects of reaching farther back
Than childhood for the steep attack
Of rhyme upon the placid eye
And language upon memory.
Approaching death your Muse danced on,
Obsessed with the quotidian,
Your verses gave their minute plots
Slim, dandified, accoustic knots,
Like form and content shaking hands,
The tactful wink such truck demands,
And rhyme was never far below
The Stygian, unbroken flow
Of dark subconsciousness that fed
An even darker fountainhead.
If you, armed with such exellence,
Could not succeed in making sense
Of this profusion what chance is
There now for any synthesis?
Although you gave a hint with your
Austerely textured metaphor
Of what might lie beyond the screen
You never could quite swear you'd seen
The Concrete Universals that
So frightened the Platonic Bat.
Now you are dead and we are left
With plunder from heroic theft,
The knick-knacks of the gods, the sights

That shape our visual appetites,
The sounds that range beyond the eyes
And race the waves for exercise,
The irony, the beach, the rain,
The journeys on that endless train
(Our witness in the corner seat
To all that must be incomplete),
And still-lives with imagined fruit
That burgeoned on the absolute
And ripened with a general love
That now, for us, must be enough.